T0160678

THE SPOONLIGHT INSTITUTE

THE SPOONLIGHT INSTITUTE

ALAN BERNHEIMER

ADVENTURES IN POETRY | 2009

Cover photograph by Alan Bernheimer
Book design by *typeslowly*
Printed in Michigan by Cushing-Malloy, Inc.
  on Glatfelter Natures Recycled paper

Some of these poems appeared first in the following publications:
Disturbed Guillotine, Famous, Ghosting Atoms, Hills, I Saw Johnny Yesterday,
In the American Tree, Ironwood, mark(s), Poetics Journal, Provincetown Poets,
Sal Mimeo, Shiny, Streets and Roads, The Best American Poetry 2004,
The Chicago Review, The Paris Review, The Sienese Shredder, The World,
This, Tramen, Up Late, and *Zzyzzyva.* Many thanks to the editors.

AIP and the author also would like to thank the publishers of his books:
Café Isotope (Geoff Young, The Figures, 1980); *State Lounge* (Lyn Hejinian,
Tuumba, 1981); *Billionesque* (Geoff Young, The Figures, 1999).

Adventures in Poetry titles are distributed to the trade through
Zephyr Press by Consortium Book Sales and Distribution [cbsd.com]
& SPD [www.spdbooks.org].

ISBN 978-09761612-8-8
adventuresinpoetry.com

CONTENTS

for Melissa

THE OPPOSITE OF PROUST

Old families last not three oaks
but stave off elimination
with endless paper and unmatched shoes

seeing film stars everywhere
set big machinery in motion

and never know what to do
in the presence of heartbreak

Could success amount to nothing
more than showing off
particles of the world?

Swaps, caps, floors, and costless collars —
they're not real
and too many eggs in that basket
are not performing

Errors approach infinite sparseness
as the Lord raptures your hand
and the way up is rounded and slow

with small lamps at the clearance points
for the unknown relation between objects and beings

AS YOU MAY KNOW

Every man's senses cue his observatory
— Charles Peirce

It may be possible to do
without dancing entirely
as far as time goes

with tendency to have things happen
Look upon this plastic life of nature
or the hegemony of baritones

and lift the steaming herd
above a still landscape
engraved by Greek upon gems

I've got to have results
to hide the details under
and remember every time

like stations of the cross
The rabbit always thinks
it is fascinating the anaconda

but what is the good
of making mistakes
if you don't use them

to distinguish former glory
from sunrise in a rear view mirror
or a bad day at the office

Melancholy is the new irony
to make sense of people
like offstage scenery

before all this technology
used an eye widener on
the sleep of reason

One swing unsphered in a void
and perspectives in graphite
dissolve to the opening sequence

THE EMBEDDED SELF

No one sees farther into a generalization than his own
knowledge of detail extends
— William James

Only that
which is absent
can be imagined
to await
the thickness of things
like birds entangled
by their feet

Big decisions
should be made
over little bottles
and squelch
the small town Inge
with dark amazement

He was
no friend to water
but let the train of events
get away
in a dime a dance world
where days are numbered

despite Esperanto
        by unwanted rest
                with cold awful dues

to pay
      Security isn't interested
               in all this confusion
sleep depravity
        or political prawns
                while satisfying lifelong dreams

drives a souvenir pluriverse
          through sleeveless errands
                    to handle and fold

DIRECTIONS FOR FIVE POEMS

for Michael Friedman

I.

Apparent statement of fact with an eyebrow-raising fillip

Apposite claim or dare in monosyllables

Personalize

Pick up thread and tie new knot

Make me a believer

Charade

Let in some air

Particularize in threes

Novelty

Trapeze

II.

Melodramatic tautology

Start recurring subtext

Borrowed phrase

Bid for immortality

Make that mortality

Begin again without adjectives

Partial truth

Syncopated argument

New lease on life (don't explain)

History

Weather

III.

Disturbing similarities

Goes without saying

Embarrassed retraction

Eye on the ball

Move heaven and earth

False conclusion (from Western Civ.)

Strong emotion recollected in tranquility . . . duh

Hit parade in sprung rhythm

Medium rare

IV.

Universal belief, reflected in particular habit

A line drive to left

Interview with a doppelganger

Ghost of a chance

Demonstrate power of words with political football

Replace four nouns and three prepositions

Win popularity contest without promising anything

Insert early memory here

What about now?

Throw a low blow

(Skating)

Poker face

Go for broke

V.

Welcome mat

Tried but true

Words without music

Where to go from here

Time out of mind

MY BLUE HAWAII

Every queen loves a lobster
with the nerve to kill time
since it's easy to be sure in a bistro
where more than dogs are turned away

Your mother had the particle
but key words are too brittle
to warp the probity of a lifetime
for a perp walk through a wafer fab

If you don't pay attention
to the little things
the big things will fall down

It's only a pay per view moon
and slowness makes everything royal

PIECE OF CAKE

Mouse traps and ping pong balls
minus contravention of nemesis

For that matter
lint used to be your clothes

and any longevity
won't come from how to know

the answer to everything
with the defects of its qualities

I hate to tell you this but
beware the sweetness of things

or epitaph time will strike
you right between the eyes

like seven more Rockettes
fluorescent with ambition

Everyone's childhood
is a psychological martini

with the qualities of its defects
running out into the sand

SLEEP CITY SQUEEGEE

Words have the same
consistency as images
in all their instars

as if sentimental chameleons
lavished thicker sunlight
once the horizon disappears

and powder of sympathy
navigates the real world
made of real words

champagne and salted almonds
over and over again
in a hail of bullets

Nobody knows
what kind of trope is
has your name on it

but glance on a great stir
This then was now
We can screenscrape it in

ZOOM

What
makes
you
better

makes
me
better
too.

"Me"
asks
too
much,

asks
for
much
love,

for
your
love,
not

your
life.
Not
that

life
is
that
great.

Is
it
great?
Doesn't

it
suck?
Doesn't.
No.

Suck
life.
No
taste?

Life
can
taste
sweet.

Can
this
sweet
time,

this
blink
time,
just

blink
and
just
end?

And
what
end
then?

What
would
then
be?

Would
we
be
through?

We
crawl
through
it,

crawl
around
it
because

"around"
and
"because"
sound

and
feel
sound
enough,

feel
like
enough.
Done.

I
left
done
for —

left
you,
for
what?

PRIOR ART SPRAY

for Lyn Hejinian

The world just appears
due to the ignorance of sentient beings
and the usual dachshund in dotted swiss
thickly settled for a measured mile

Even shapes must have a likeness
how puppets dream of being human
in this filmic backwater

where elderly princesses sit
in little pools of deportment
regarding the blue of birds

Ideas take the place of sorrow
indistinguishable as larches
letting the clock run out
on the you/me phenomenon

The crazier the people you are sleuthing out
the nearer you are to an end of trouble
with bunches of glum airmen
moving in diplomatic circles

Leaves brush open a star
as the tide plants a kiss on the shore

I read: therefore I think:
grim twinkle, skid in the shot

The logic of the gloomy woman
made radiant by artificial light
was inevitably to retreat

DEPARTMENT NINE

Email and epiphany target one's person
to begin with
          all the time in the world
for ab- and other -ilities

The regime is coup-proof
We get what we need from arithmetic
and floozies with Uzis
           dance like yourself
on fixed abode

It takes two to make eyes meet
this side of crazy
         instead of
    a spark in ether
real tinsel and nonpareils

     in a voice full of money

Your socks will still disappear
with used atoms
         and men left on

20 QUESTIONS

What can be said of the unspeakable that has not already been unsaid

What kind of pill does it take

Is outliving enemies a hollow victory

Can moonlight prevent the leaves from stirring

How many presidents say "nucular" instead of "nuclear"

Is the brain constructed from activity

How is life on the natch

Is solid eye contact critical to being a hit

Who would fardels bear

What is the statute of limitations

Do you know you've arrived when carts are free

Do we get all the help we need from arithmetic

Who is as tickled as a dog with two dicks

Does something for everyone mean nothing for anyone

Would you be kind enough

How many light bulbs does it take to change the world

Are you in this for the overalls

Do fine feathers make fine birds

Remember when a million was a billion

Can what they call civilization be right if people mayn't die
    in the room where they were born

THE SPOONLIGHT INSTITUTE

Days, like fingers, unfold their battalions
— Paul Éluard

1.

I'm tired of being so dismantled
decidedly thudless on hidden springs

when the world always has
an explanation for itself

going in and out of the woodwork
Will it hurt the picture

to make the ether hideous?
Longing leads the past

around to the present and
suddenly some subtle entity

vulnerable to too much time
is supposed to shrink your wig

Why monetize the anomie
and still go through shoes at this age

where nothing is too much trouble
Decisions aren't made

less likely by flash bulbs
less fascinating than floor shows

subsiding into hygiene
eliminate guesswork by speaking

in the language of things
as power messaging creates

a hormone cocktail in your prospects
courtesy of Freud

the spectral getting practical
for a fundamentally bad egg

2.

Is this supposed to be a movie?
The only secrets are taken to the grave

where everyone knows anything
to put everything in perspective

gets ironic in no time
Good hinges make such sad metaphors

with prepositions akimbo
and suchness is no stranger

nose in the cosmos
to alibi glamor

that has a way with thugs
like relativity to a railroad

No matter what folded maps
just barely illustrate memory

all the future does is spoil the present
or change your longitude

to the furtive lands
and look into thought colored eyes

The flight of geese through the drowsy mind
is conducive to sleep

as evening to a caveman
underlaps a substitute world

reminiscent of mist
but studded by intention

to illuminate the air
with eponymous bird

3.

Personality is only a persistent error
to mope like a monument

where cooking takes the place of thought
and the geezer keeps coming back for more

We felt our names erased by peculiarity
as if the mask itself were speaking

about perfection of experience
We moved beyond the need for fact

by access to power
how nomad detectors fuel deal fever

and the satisfactory inexpensiveness of nowhere
seemed like a hand on your heart

or an outward sign of intended bleak
the horizon dissolving at dusk

Eternity of desire is
the bright side of oblivion

whichever comes first
since puppy love bebop madness

has no lessons for the eventless
and things bite back when fascination wears off

The early universe was perfectly fluid
but there isn't as much standby

as there used to be
when the public preferred

their screens silent and
age is replaced by possessions

4.

You've picked up a lot of camping
tricks in the margin of error

legally blind to the nondescript
fluttering home through the half light

much less fun
than chain smoking roll your owns

or a soiled dove
taking shade on borrowed time

or come as your pet aversion
with a houndstooth lining

and no big eyes
left of boom

unpeel like animals
but back to the inventory
Don't get me started
on nervous sleep

accelerating interest in comfort
Say goodbye to meticulous

at humanity's loading dock
The imaginary future

replaces the real one
and delays mood episodes

subtracting adverbs from used literature
with epic as the new awesome

walking through lightning
and other people's dreams

5.

Moving among gnomes
outdoes a blind spot for irony

weak on verbs
the familiar false

as a touchstone
Life is short to go to work

and premeditate the next thought
you're not putting

that atom juice on me
with a word to the wires

that diminish appetite for magnitude
in any kite wind

the mystery of someone else
or remembered wallpaper

just the same as it is in Cincinnati
angling for fiasco

A sentimental nature is welcome
to cheap stunts

that makes things matter
if inside know-how

summons the equipment
to hollow victory

expecting anything
of a stranger

too fast to live
too young to happy

6.

Dreamy improvs lubricate
the machinery of fate

the way sarcasm is a little
out of place in the jungle

cornerless as an end in sight
It's time to move the furniture

but I am not the person to see
about that event horizon

or even think of uncertainty
underneath everything

Since aliens ate my brain
numerous sounds of English

make room for occasional tables
and sudden behavior

the world needs pills against
The worst part's almost over now

that fresh pictures take
steps to smooth maps

while we noodle a glut of tuneage
and the star boarder

dreams of electric soup
I am past work

capital being crystallized labor
so it's okay to blank out

the whole kit and caboodle
One monkey don't start the show

GRAVITY ROAD

There are no rocking chairs in hell
I took the tour last week
Now I just want to browse
              dig tunnels
                build bridges
                    move mountains

Let nature do the heavy work

My rule of thumb
Is sleight of hand
And long of tooth

              Spotless is my name

Sensational crude essence
Fills the zoning envelope

              Tab fields exit pupil

They're going to bench test your dive
And empty bottles absolve you of particularity

One day bumps the next
The things that befall
Words are accidence

Fire
   escapes romance
       the air

Affection unabated
In any scrape

Say uncle who motions dismay
For the time being gravity takes heart in

AGAINST NATURE

A man watches and waits
while we watch this man
and wait for what
he is waiting for

We become familiar
with the majority of numbers
under a hundred

At home in effort
he is trying
not to become food

He motions sideways
The simulacrum of narrative
usurps attention to time
Words dream of mouthfuls

Thing of night
dissolved by glee
Remarks keep slipping from transparency

His eyes are a rented blue
who cares for things
outside of enough

Liquid nails beat the pavement
Just a muscle takes sides
with no motive

Little gasoline passes
this descriptive setting
but the future appears
to advance toward us

Mild foreign body sensation
accompanies any possibility

He looks to the horizon
for enthusiasm
walking around money

The voice of waters
says burn bridges
and he smokes a cigarette
in his head

Better than wildest dream
trees slowly display the wind

WORD OF ART

First a flicker of telepathy
Then screw le mot juste
Carefully into its socket
So the electricity doesn't spill.

Act natural.
It isn't all honey for people with learning
And don't make excuses for rock.

Eye on curve, hand on lever, things on mind,
The rest of the subjects refer to you.

Words make wide open spaces.

Dissolve to perpetual motion
With time off for behavior.

The body likes its relations
Embroidering inventions
To say anything:

This music is not of my choosing.
The enormous seaminess throws a textbook punch.
But it wasn't the stars that thrilled me.

SPECIMEN OF AN INDUCTION TO A POEM

Nature especially abhors the smell of vacuums
While the spiritual
    cottager frescoes
        his crystal ball

Weak weather for a length of time

Images harbor messy affinities
Like doctors we're used to it

Once thaws gradually decline
Spring leaves trees green

Demonstrates words used as words
One breath of air
    the next of smoke

But the picture doesn't recognize me

A unit of general signal should alter fate

Your furniture is six days old
And sleep has absorbed falsehood

Resting objects
    different as eggs
Shadow thoughts

Botanical calm slips from stills

FLOREX GARDENS

for AWB

The choo-choo train passed through the fields like clockwork
day in and out, each instant carried forward against wobble that
wrung drones from harem schemes into a drowsy backstroke
down the bank of fragrance hanging over still flowers grown for
the dinner table. An oval bed of nails held the arrangement in the
half-light from an adjoining room, where perforations trained
puffs of air against metal fingers to draw Brahms from the upright.
Struck tons push the replica through ether. Promising geometry
blossoms would furnish slender future one way or another.

PERSONAL LIFE

A short fuse on a long afternoon
twinges for concentrate
as silent upholstery after illusion

the one worth fainting for

The other steps gingerly into day
distinguishing each likelihood
with a catalogue of glances

There is no bowling alley to the subconscious
as wake up fresh
   made in Italy
     designed by God
precipitates words into sight
or intention to dismay

Every panorama does good
    that outlaws willies
and belief in maps

Outtakes load the self of stardom
Canals on Mars break into print

TOPIC A

No scenery in the scenery
Attraction of fact
Puts construction on things
You have been somewhere before
Units combine plausible shade
Cloud in front, sun in back
Atoms extended in space

KIOSK

Darkness, darkness.
Then the surface pictures a scene.
"Being with her, people want to die."

All dreams contain the dreamer
whose revolving doors refer
and refer
    such figs
to vehicular sleep
    as waltz sweetly into each booth,
exchange lip stuff,
and lunch on the Mississippi.

Stop casting porosity
with a body of meaning.

Palming glances makes a party go
but angels can't
have posterity increase.

Exit the interior life
    for a stab at the gene pool —
as against
    trout ventilation service,
    touching a drop,
wrought oxygen.

It's hard on the heels of love
that unrest victims combat philosophy
trapped by self and moving
                    parts
upside possibility from mouths of how.

A BOTTLE IN THE SMOKE

The beach remains a tiny piece of the world.
Who is playing opposite one
                feeling for objects
comes down with sight.

Fundamental granularity is so lovely,
why are the balconies missing?

Enough choices don't use much virtue
and little misbehavior passes
                through such big hands
as red dots stitch fancy in blue sky.

The hard time is for not telling.
The trick is to see
                whose heart's gone
trouting in a newspaper boat.

NATURE

The field needs a window
to give onto it
   and of itself
a view of smoke

distinguishing particles
as from afar
   as from a farm
with perfect handwringing

and dilapidated guesses
who is there
   for who knows
what season

alternating earnestly
in memory of
   special felt
delicatessen genes

with perfect handwriting
as a charge for personality
   and ventures beyond
the funny house

so eliminate the star
qua stranger
   that buffers
anonymity pills

that dualism is forlorn
for native speakers
   in the first
blush of omnium.

APPLE OF EYE

Only trees keep up with memory's enlargement
the way
       gasoline evaporates
miles into the landscape

and we need to asterisk out love obtained by philtre.

Loads of self pause for hold music,
head for heights, observe radio silence

with hooks to Renoir eyes.

The dying heart can only march
across the wide museum,
promising dances on railroad time

now that mental means modern again.

Stolen hours are the sweetest
sleep
     while God abhors a naked
singularity in the gymnasium of wind.

Fine doings cast future light cones
                 between jobs
and the doings of fine men,

alive and talking to strangers.
The play of fruit upon
the retina is sensuous by itself.

POEM

pieces of me
who is without doubt
slow in pockets
promise natural shades

code of honor
code of dots
consolidated Edison
what are you asking from?

prepare to be amazed
wardens of autumn
components look familiar
between frauleins

out of fame:
why they see sin
here you are in Marseilles
among the watermelons

take those airplanes off
I couldn't see the balconies
for the balconies
things in terms of words

control top hose
Kafka on mushrooms
Kafka on microwaves
data on your seats

we have unity
in spades
temps with perms
the pace of a sphinx

episode recalls
the spooky scherzo
where birds retreat
to the bosoms of men

can cheap boxes talk?
objects in motion
take hot car seats
and cut grass

interim to my silo dreams
eyes rose
from the floor
and met

think up
the next compliment
skating on the wrong
side of the ice

it cracked me
all the way up
hole in the yonder
this shuddering thigh

GRANDEE OF ILLUSION

Sweet land of thee
I take my liberty
a perfect stranger
in roofless fields

Strong verbs faint
from buried reds and
folding infinity stops —
no wonder cracks slip through

Practice makes perfect specimens
but we look different
six inches apart
from life expectancy

There is a wide choice of shoes
in the bachelor's solitude
many a day off
with the same sense of enlargement

Things, time, and words
sing the telegrapher's accent
with the same enlightenment
miles from nowhere

No ship carries a man
rated spotless Christian hero
(words at the edge of memory trip
off the tongue) towards infinitely familiar shore

BILLIONESQUE

for RLK

Anything that is not analogous is all a dream
with too many cops partial to eel,
another life wreathed in smilax
peeling off the hills

Those present hear whispers
between swiftly flowing words:
boarding music, floor lighting
I could not be like that —

a dailiness bereft of aperçus
and feathered elliptical marquees
where adagio dancers come up
for air to innovate crisply

In case of rapture this car will be empty
or deep carnation
Extras are called atmosphere and
few expect statues

The beauty of it is
I am not that important either

PERMANENT WAVE

It is a nice spot
swarming with oxygen
and takes a path
of least time through space.

Geography educates the palate from hunger.
My specimens come to me:

Blue carbon paper floating
                              down blue sky
lightly crazed all over
                    and under
fleeting circumstances
there is a living in it.

Picture the author
a scenic vapor alongside,
then you have to eat your lunch alone.

Lower dimensional analogs
learn to say hello
over the plane.

Any leisure splays fate
                        seen from abroad
demanding hidden charms.

A creature of weather,
material qualms die down a little.

Though the light changes
chances are the vicinity
the familiar takes will see us through

and what has been so nice
seeing it coming.

STORM AT SEA

Here and in the distance
a whole fleet of
shoe-shaped ships

driven through the
brown whipped waves
one leaves

a wake of lime
sunlight another
pitches through

towards port
where clear skies beckon
on the horizon

flukes dwarf the ships
against earth-colored clouds
gulls veer in the wind

Meeressturm
Peter Brueghel

BEFORE DEFOE

Deep sky
Nights as a kid
Eyelids peeled

I've forgotten more
Drifting down the staggered lights
Than you'll ever know

Rhubarb, pieces of eight
Feet in the air
And the more I see

IQ getting filmy
Car lengths at a time
The more I see

Surface tension, rimfire
I need my fingers to be careful with
The more uncomfortable I get

ARE THERE BIRDS?

This is urgent
Or have I been in a bad mood for two years
Waiting to be dreamed?

A small paradise
Where a man arrives and shoots himself
Teeming with glee

Though unaccountable nervosity
Fingers little eddies in the air
Ways freaked into life

One thing is twilight
And one after another
Glows in the giddy sorrow
They fly through to you

INSIDE CHEESE

The aged gouda had grown complex, its acoustics swollen to visibility, and the sunny complexion inherited from a northern polder was laced with the whispers of photons cruising the waxy mantle of layered gloss left by each demented glance that had fallen from eyes on the brink of sleep. The brink was lurid and echoed the roar of termites from a nearby windmill. Time and again the prodigious sails swooped out of the sky like an amusement park on fire, and with each revolution the lattice lost molecules to robot bacteria whose cousins had long since polished milk to a half life in the low gear rotunda.

LOVE AND JOURNALISM

Head's continuous toss a slight yank from behind, hank in hands,
his and hers, lefts, right to the coffee. A profession of delivery.
Composed for the rectangle. Over the shoulder look. Cup brim
over nose. Fingers learn to handle. Eyes in their corners give
thought to the part type plays.

LETTER

Marseilles

This brilliant artificial knee, spring-hinged with small birds' bones, is too late, and the books on metallurgy, hydroponic farming, and beekeeping were sent to the wrong country.

The money belt is useless (unless a sailor will buy it) — the room costs 10 francs a day, with doctors, and I haven't stood up in weeks. Huge varicose veins map my treks through the Sudan, where hot winds dry up white men from the inside. A year there ages one as much as four elsewhere.

At night I smell the harbor and thick, yellow moonlight falls across my bed. I sleep no more than an insect.

Give me the news.

Rimbaud

LIQUID STEEL

stuffy maybe and they say a calmness
sandwiched between reserve layers
of blue cotton as much as there is
a shower of droplets looking liquid

what if there's nothing going on? what
if lassa fever breaks out? what if
outer space is forever hostile
or a dragon does swallow the sun?

the facets of mathematics the
way numbers turn up like blossoms
leverage on your nail clipper
or your teabag spinning and dripping

so much is in the mail at one time
we could borrow this permanent
floating world or even its smell
like the thought of acrobats

in the air turning in too much
to snails and cyclones on a pinhead
honed by idiots to the point
where it punctures the skin

TREMOR OF INTENT

The peripheral beckons
like a mouse on fire
and gee the water looks good

to it too
Such ratios twinkle
by themselves

as I am lucky to be an inch
taller in the morning
by the way
         than at night

more than willing then
to see impetuous details too
small for lips
         hanging on your words

AMARILLO

I hear the sentimental music dying
that makes my helmet ring
　　　　　— Blaise Cendrars

I was born alive
the sky was all you could see
eating and running
a part from a world

rendered obsolete by the violin
granular lubricity the equivalent
of gravity streaming past limbs
and torso

　　　　watch my smoke
give me a perch　　I'm not talking
while the flavor lasts　　listen to
the sugar pour

　　　　　　along the rim
　　　　　　word of mouth
now this
and now this

　　　　　is what I call crisp
New York is a department of the sticks
chicken today feathers tomorrow
you can't see because it's radio

traffic draws away from you
on specular fire   eyes smart
not good at what not like
ill at ease in the offing

you are "it" as is
viscera means iceberg
that wasn't no buffalo
that was thunder

a raving beauty at the turn
of the century known for its
helium and silhouette of beef
hoofing the horizon

much feasting little fun
lunar gaffes of benzedrine proportions
wings cross in consequence of air
you are allowed to copy the weather

keys in one pocket change
in another say hello
to the phone who are
sure of dinner

at the back of the mind
when it rains it shines
landscape
            as nature intended

nothing is sweeter than figs
but it's nice to drink the water
words row across the surface of
oo la la or snorkle

what is known by heart
as the glass harmonica
absorbs loss like champagne
and the streets are music to police

I am descended from my ancestors
hare brained antics freeze
my tears in their tracks
where the anchovies spawn

a domino of light from the rear
view mirror across the eyes
falling as the dusk idly
disappears on the road ahead

circulation drops hardly stir
the odor of fragility
is the weight that it carries
talking through altitude

handwriting cures personality
some roles played by ideas
the language of mechanics
gives the hand a head

it is a sunny day and
no mountain stood a chance
of more neighborhood
emulsifying vitreous humor

early tensile flyleaves
at the edge of valence
faint from farsight
one routine is pulling teeth

off also rans
the last dinosaur turns back
for a blink at the ginkgo
with a weakness for feet

chiefly diehard furlongs
feeling vapors
                    drop away
shy on geography

I started out younger
all over the place
merely sportive slippers
thought a sign of decadence

to dispel abandon they ate the experiment
on ladyfingers at the end
of thirst a close shave with an
afterthought

                    business end overboard
no such animal
                    out on a spree
is a nuisance

like the feel of imminent wealth
drills through night
every favorite tree
occurs to a silkworm

those geographers know how to travel
long on luck
short on luxury
lucky in love's one track mind

underarms are circling overhead
outbreaks of innocence dot the map
with clouds of baby powder
childhood ends when the dog blurs

and the blush dies away
to vestigial foghorns
relieved of decisions
they make themselves

cautious to a fault
orphans to be
live on thousands a year
limber and chagrined

nearly posthumous certainty
forms the meniscus
big molecules draw flies
natives burnish the lapels

shall we stroll into focus
bereft of octane
population eyes only
elevation byo

drogue chutes popped first
initials at large
envelop their own gyros
frantic in amber as

cigarets keep gloves apart
once any stint beckons
foreground to impudence
of each an equal amplifier

take the heat as casualty
semibreves minims crotchets quavers
there was age and space
crank the awning up

a rash of mileage
weekend p.m. lull
for want of cordials
there is more than one Carolina

Chickadee combing telephone
wires stranded in fugue
I was touched
you want to leave something

to hang thc botanicals on
and evidence snaps up the extra
far back behind the groceries
a passion for optics

diamondback terrapin in its day
took care of the afternoon
tandem red brick diagonals
wound up on an arm of the sea

get results in person
gas is more hedgy
where the hero is arch
room approaching body

temperature instead of intelligence
architecture shadows this man's world
delicate in its feathered coinage
and ornamental hermits

close calls are their specialty
mustering hairline watermarks
whose incandescent dewpoint
furnishes the mirage

what is enough
practically displays elements
bordering on dismay
myself included

A CANNIBAL FINDS A FORK IN THE ROAD

He is lying or telling the truth
He knows the missionaries will lie

The village lies to the left and the right
The fork is in his mind
The missionary is already on the fork

Even the road is gone

PORTRAIT OF A MAN

Your face fills the sky
like a windmill
with the look of living certainty
and a smile dissolved by air

You sit on your shoulders

We see hair, mouth
the nose on your face
and the light brown
light in your brown
fifteenth century eyes
one looking inside
the other ahead

You wear black
the color of the universe
and the blue sky is white in back

What we don't know
is what you are about to say

Portait of a Man
Hans Memling

AVAILABLE LIGHT

You are all your friends have in common
just as coffee brings civilization to its day
Certain boundaries are crossed
and expect to be recrossed
or your diplomatic immunity vanishes with your sleeve of watches
As for everybody a class of objects comes to attention
What you don't notice is the weight it is comfortable to sleep under
What you do is the possibility for coincidence
agitated as if you were a magnet
Nobody minds bothering to see this magic
interesting the days in the week for instance
but forgets with pangs of familiarity
or a sudden shyness stumbles in
The life you are leading numbs me with its glee
How can you find Haydn depressing?

OR SOMETHING

You think the day is made of time
Like a field of four o'clocks
I live in this city to cross the street
To my heart's content
Or something
The same luminosity
As the sky: eastern buildings
For a few minutes after sunset
And buy some fluke for dinner

CAFÉ ISOTOPE

Wind light

Empirical background

The birds are sure flying low today
As a part of me fingers forever

But really they find no mistake
Earmarked overnight virtuoso

Deliquescence plays havoc in cahoots with but

What special virtue this room has
I'm sure I don't know

Very local outright risk
Owing illusion to
Earn a living

Pipe dreams to singing lariat

SPINAL GUARD

for Louis Postel

No snow falls from blue sky
with the effortless slide of the trombone

Besides, the blind drive slow
with the nonchalance of boys

and uncanny gentleness empties
the planetarium into the street
courtesy of Mozart
who detested the flute

eager, destitute, a/k/a Wolf
his secret slang the wind

Some spectacular fish for pets
and afterwards infinite novelty, clinging

Versus three meals a day, knockout drops,
frankly hopeless downtown fever

RIPOLIN

Wood pins clothes on the line
particularly now the wind is blowing

so mothballs evaporate a mile or more away
and frost X-rays car hoods

Who heard music? The grief is brilliant

retinal pulse, virtually asterisks
on the face of visceral pastimes

For a little while perhaps ten hours
have passed one after the other

CARAPACE

The face of a stranger
is a privilege to see
each breath a signature
and the same sunset fifty years later
though familiarity is an education

who likes what most?

high rounded cornices with baby
moon hubcaps played by the wind

electricity travels from time
to time on the surface of these lips

thoroughly tropical pleasure
forms the customary features
combination eyeteeth and semaphore

everything I touch turns
to flesh or vice versa

VISIBLE MEANS

Here for now a small wonder
tea's velvet tongue on fluted teeth

nobody's fault prevents the poor
from being born, with spectators

no wonder foreign objects
contrary to light
touch and go numb
possibly people or plants

half indoors, top half outside
seeing stars at the edge of insomnia
and gray apples at dawn

number, uneasy and underfoot
in some lifelong radio outskirts

VENTRILOQUY

Splendid
waking midday drowning or walleyed
ready to hate

when each eardrum heartbeat fly lines
down French curves in Mozart Avenue
to solos birds peel off the sky
green with its bruises of light

and pillowing high babies
whose cheeks invent the wind
that is philosophy to my ears

The altitude of the far
shore is tremendous
half reflection and unforeshortened

by surfeit of instant
like a river of mercury
run through a lawn of chives

unsung by felicitous memory
revenging stringy dreams
unable to tell them apart

PASSING STRANGE

Blunt good looks cut out day
patterned after strides through nerve

No accident the sky clouds
figure is envelope blue

dovetails with appetite
It sounds like it

Weather is personal equation
and existing light jolts small fortune
by weight of characteristic

What I think I hear are words
lost in plain sight
though details feel passing fancy
with binocular relief

Material needs a life of fact
to make a spectacle of
one of these days

from STATE LOUNGE

Buntline special

"For Newton space and time was the sense organ of God."

— Feyerabend

cows in the cornfield

Blood is liquid flesh.

pulling up to the 40th parallel

A flourish at the end of a signature to guard against forgery is a paraph.

leapfrog with weather

The seams in the human skull are known as brahma, for their resemblance to Hindi characters.

bridges freeze first

Bedouins sharpen their vision by painting the whites of their eyes blue.

and perfusion

The twinkling of stars is caused by a rapidly moving pattern of caustic surfaces passing the eye.

why cars move in waves, is it humans in them

Systems whose properties are dependent upon their previous histories are said to exhibit hysteresis.

interest the traffic will bear

The svaha is the lapse between lightning and thunder.

turnpike

Between the first hello and the goodnight kiss comes the svaha.

PARTICLE ARMS

Particle Arms was first produced by Poets Theater at Studio Eremos, San Francisco, in November 1982. It was directed by Nick Robinson and designed by Johanna Drucker, with lights by Jean Day. The cast:

Karp	Tom Mandel
Bunker	Steve Benson
Nyla	Eileen Corder
Fictitious Doe	Kit Robinson
Liguras	Stephen Rodefer
Old Man	Tinker Greene
Old Woman	Melissa Riley

Scene 1

(Night, a city street)

KARP: How about a nip of distress? Thrill your spine with a piece of info. Why travel 3,000 miles to change mosquitoes?

BUNKER: Dispatch the wranglers at will. I stand on my footsteps, and overheard menaces melt into my cocktails. Reverbs concentrate the mix.

KARP: Will chin factor deliver curved fire to pocket gophers on regular basis?

BUNKER: That's what's known as nobody's business. The horizon describes a circle of miles, a far cry from old days, snoopy eyes on the road ahead. I wonder if you'd like to tell me a joke.

KARP: I'm a relative of humor. These are the shoes that try men's soles.

BUNKER: You have survived, and that is enough for now. Continental air behaves independently.

KARP: It's tricky being typical of yourself. The air is always at variance with the temperature. Should I be punished for being born with a high IQ?

BUNKER: The real man is absent minded. Around the corner, the wind's from Venice. I have a sudden thirst for wine and shallots.

KARP: A kiss for the cook. Tremolos call for every diagnosis, and you never know why you don't get a life supply. Imagine your teeth in a mirror.

BUNKER: Life is an obligation which friends often owe each other in the wilderness.

KARP: Enjoy woods with precision compass, watch cops equitate, look forward to new habit, combine teenage emotions with present day thought.

BUNKER: I have lived here for several phone books, and expect more than a slap in the face with a frozen chicken. There is a mashed landscape beneath this asphalt. I'm waiting for a chance to slip away.

KARP: Making fun of science by marching through fields. You prefer a supple to an accretive or staccato logic?

NYLA: (*Off*) Thank you for the dance, Captain. These two-steps are getting a little stiff. (*Enters*) I can hardly get over my voice. It's six weeks since you sent your laundry out. You must be in love.

BUNKER: You're talking with your mouth open.

NYLA: I merely wanted to take you on the wing.

KARP: If I could do cartwheels I would.

BUNKER: If you have something to say, lower your voice and smile.

NYLA: Don't look so injudicious. I always get the point of jokes. The directions are based on material prepared by Uncle Sam. Life has a good effect on me.

KARP: And it does its tricks.

BUNKER: The name's familiar, like putting your pants on. But they don't make that kind of time on watches. Peculiar risk of harm masks the clench.

NYLA: Don't hurt yourself to change the subject.

KARP: He thinks I'm from National Geographic. My work here has always been volunteer work. Cash is mere bouquet.

NYLA: Money is the sex of arithmetic.

BUNKER: The illusion is that everything is the same. Heavy machinery in the backwash of the Milky Way. It's not my country. It isn't even luxury.

KARP: Suit yourself. Assuage the turbulence of rational awareness.

NYLA: My personality does not evaporate. There are times I need a ballad, but the feeling is not for your amusement. Someone your shape shouldn't wear those shades. I'm having a hard enough time with underlings without contributions from the bemused. Minerals thrive on benevolent neglect, while biology sheds a tear for the uninvited. You opted for a limited scenario.

On-the-job habits become dream metaphors. Now
you spend nights touching up days, a little twist here
and there, up and down the chain of command.

KARP: I'm having vicissitudes right now.

BUNKER: Don't mention it.

NYLA: A man goes far on what he thinks he's going to get.

KARP: You cannot predict the world you will need.

BUNKER: No hard feelings.

NYLA: Since we have so little anesthesia we rely upon vanity.

KARP: You can tell the umps are out of town. *(More and more
             aside)* Primitive man gets to know things mostly by
             pretending to be them.

BUNKER: I need to hear words.

NYLA: Our fervors were dulled by the comforts of the
             veranda.

KARP: Dead burrito bites gutter dust.

BUNKER: The body doesn't lie.

KARP: The coffee rings xerox well today.

NYLA: Skin is rarely busy.

KARP: The music of the vocal cords is a language to itself.

BUNKER: I had to use a muscleman to get me off the floor.

NYLA: It's no accident.

BUNKER: You're the doctor.

NYLA: Too small for words.

BUNKER: Our history is an emergency. Handsome couples
             pigment the neighborhood. Give me something to
             sleep.

NYLA: Light stretched thin as radio accounts for night.
             Otherwise stars melt over everything.

KARP: These big quiet spots frighten me.

BUNKER: Brightness falls from the air halfway through another
             day. Somebody always sees big footsteps. Stilts are no
             excuse.

KARP: Why play hard to get by yourself?

NYLA: Don't traipse into marasmus.

BUNKER: Tip my mitt to that custard? Get those curves out
             of here. Charm is a little crease beneath the eyes.
             It's hard finding people that don't take advantage
             of familiarity. See what happens when the unsaid
             gets said? I don't have experience at this. I don't have

time off for behavior. Private life seems pallid, but it keeps a civil tongue in your head. I don't need rabbits coming out of my ears. The unemployed words largely outnumber the employed. I've been from several places, and I'm going to be from here. *(Exit)*

KARP: Queasiness rolls down bravado like window shades.

NYLA: Aw, turn blue.

Scene 2

(Another town, hotel lobby)

FICTITIOUS DOE: Fictitious Doe woke with a start. Er, excuse me. What do I do now? Liguras ignored him. Business as usual. Imaginative ways with a toothpick. My acquaintance is a combination of features, foreign but sweet.

LIGURAS: *(Cold shoulder)*

FIC DOE: I'd like to speak to one of your swamis.

LIGURAS: This man is making that horrible noise.

FIC DOE: I'll take my chances with a dose of primordial hiss. I was a phenomenal modernist.

LIGURAS: Ham and eggs.

FIC DOE: I was just dreaming two lively nocturnal pastels —

clear skies, except for a few cumulus marionettes. Fictitious Doe was flying from piano wires over scenery air only knew about.

LIGURAS: Do you really like these amoebae?

FIC DOE: Daily life holds no great attraction for me. The tree is a newspaper item. I'll sleep in empty units.

LIGURAS: Treat yourself to a minute on the lazy Susan. The sidelight brings: out dimensions, but your timing is a fraction off. Intent to cause. Offensive touching is enough. Your eyes are filmed by passing years. Bourgeois means have a nice trip. Ethical suicide would be one alternative.

FIC DOE: Money isn't everything.

LIGURAS: People use it sometimes.

FIC DOE: I'm too light for heavy work and too heavy for light work.

(Enter Old Couple)

OLD MAN: Joe does floor material slow.

OLD WOMAN: Some of the donors are actually cadavers.

LIGURAS: Ice box talk.

OLD MAN: The electric lights are back in their sockets.

OLD WMN: He must be using it for blood.

(*Exit Old Couple*)

LIGURAS: Realistic speech makes the world go away.

FIC DOE: I got a swiss cheese back.

LIGURAS: I believe it.

FIC DOE: Words failed Fictitious Doe — an actor's nightmare. He was consumed by tactile feedback.

LIGURAS: I don't mean to carp, but you're leaving dirt.

FIC DOE: Fictitious Doe had something on his mind. I have things on my mind.

LIGURAS: One huge stammer.

FIC DOE: If your thinking does something you don't want it to, you should be able to say something microscopic. Entertaining doubts is a lost cause, short-lasted at best. But my feet are always treading Jell-O.

LIGURAS: Be executive.

FIC DOE: Teeth waltz down my throat.

LIGURAS: Divine wind makes the species visible.

(*Enter Old Couple*)

89

OLD MAN: They've finally figured out how humans get around.

OLD WMN: Gummed reinforcements give you a run for your money.

OLD MAN: I'm keeping my eyes open for a sandwich.

OLD WMN: It wasn't the stars that thrilled me.

LIGURAS: No fooling.

FIC DOE: Lips print a tissue that corrects the weather, lulled by the weight of public opinion. My downfall was a trampoline catastrophe.

OLD WMN: Nise pipple.

OLD MAN: A hero needs sleep. Tollbooth optimism —

LIGURAS: He thinks he's something on a stick.

OLD MAN: — shouldn't happen to a berg.

OLD WMN: Any leisure we had, we spent knitting khaki mufflers.

            (*Exit Old Couple*)

LIGURAS: His better half better have her head examined.

FIC DOE: Fictitious Doe wondered what class he was. I suppose it's just me. But I was inoculated against island fever. I feel eyes dancing on my face.

LIGURAS: You are protected by the enormity of your stupidity.

(*Enter Bunker*)

LIGURAS: Park your back hoe.

BUNKER: Watch my smoke.

FIC DOE: Er, mister nice guy becomes nasty wise guy.

BUNKER: Scared money always loses. And I'm not feeling very
             particular. The loose surface of the earth is soil. Give
             me someplace to sleep.

LIGURAS: Why bother? You have been somewhere before.

BUNKER: I flap terribly. Dip your brights or pine away.

LIGURAS: I've got a clean roster.

BUNKER: Then prevent foreign object damage. Embalmed beef
             is not a regularity favorite.

LIGURAS: There is a vacancy in the dumbwaiter.

BUNKER: Let the student magnet have it. My practice is the
             roof. Meteors crowd the night the other side of the
             clouds.

LIGURAS: Take a dream.

FIC DOE: Fictitious Doe turned his back on two fronts. I've got to be myself somehow. I'm here to think on my feet. Speech is a matter of the mouth making gestures.

BUNKER: Trouble seeing double? Close one eye.

LIGURAS: A case of panache.

(*Enter Old Couple*)

OLD WMN: Every picture is sick.

OLD MAN: The deepest navy in the west.

LIGURAS: Get a load of those shots.

OLD WMN: It's different when you read it in the paper.

OLD MAN: Every American expects an interview.

BUNKER: There ought to be a license. A foot stands for a footprint. So many people still say so. It is clear what you do. It sounds like it. Time was weather got better. Now drivers push cars. Their word is enough.

OLD MAN: Welcome to the nineteenth century.

BUNKER: When I crashed the legion I ditched the past.

OLD WMN: It's all smoked meat now.

Scene 3

(Next morning)

FIC DOE: *(Rifling Bunker's suitcase)* Unguarded moments put logic in mothballs. I should have been a mechanical drawer. Light waves keep us in line. You lost the vacuum attachment.

LIGURAS: The rush of air it creates causes blindness. Grammar is pushing cells around, but the tables take time to turn. We're out of eradicator.

FIC DOE: Wads of detail. I have a small business of my own, and I like being someone who's who.

LIGURAS: Don't strain your personality. *(To Old Couple)* Meet the new boss.

OLD MAN: There's something fishy in this world.

OLD WMN: Being poor is sanitary.

FIC DOE: Hocus pocus.

BUNKER: *(Entering)* The new order still preens?

OLD WMN: *(Reminiscing)* We'd eat powders out of envelopes.

BUNKER: That's wonderful stuff you have on. I depend on my friends to recognize me. Has anybody seen my grip?

OLD WMN: The picture looks better when you're here.

FIC DOE: I'm at a loss to say.

LIGURAS: Search me.

BUNKER: Someone's playing with live rounds.

FIC DOE: I don't know the first thing about specifications.

LIGURAS: Us sidewalk superintendents mind our business. I can't afford to wind up pushing buttons.

FIC DOE: The quadratic formula escapes me too.

OLD MAN: At my age the dog has its own car.

BUNKER: I'm going to count to one. At that point the luggage reappears. . . . One.

OLD WMN: (*Finding case*) Inanimate objects survive upheavals.

BUNKER: (*To Old Couple*) Grab a bite, both of you. I hold the central nervous system in respect. Everything else is strut. Hmmm. Idle hands have filtered my belongings. I'll thank their owner to put 'em up.

LIGURAS: Keep your lid on.

BUNKER: Let's take a look at the goldfish. (*Exit with Liguras*)

FIC DOE: Eyes choose what to see. Time for a plunge. Don't get fat. (*Exit*)

OLD WMN: What do you expect?

OLD MAN: A moment's respite. What we have in our hands is already enough.

OLD WMN: Yes, but we must avoid anything that tends to destroy the illusion of nature. No editor can be trusted not to spoil a diary. Natives nowadays choose what they drop for the anthropologist close at their heels.

OLD MAN: What is science but the absence of prejudice backed by the prescience of money? When it rains all houses seem to slant, but we are no closer to detecting despondency in a test tube.

OLD WMN: All the same, the commotion of imbeciles gives a jukebox organization to the experiment, without which eggs are considerably too scrambled. I shouldn't be surprised at a breakthrough before long.

OLD MAN: We can derive a maximum of attention from our cover, while mouth parts mime the content of speech. (*Hears steps approach*) Keep the aspidistra flying.

FIC DOE: (*Enters*) Events adopt a breakneck air. The Lone Ranger has justice by the throat. My pension is around the next comer. (*Fondling stolen rabbit's foot*)

OLD WMN: Mounting delusion insulates the panic button.

FIC DOE: Rubberneckers have a funny way of getting snapped. (*Hides rabbit's foot among Liguras's belongings*)

OLD MAN: Age enjoys the privilege of fuzzy likeness. Oh!

BUNKER: (*Entering with Liguras*) The principal damage was to his other shirt — a tissue of alibis that wouldn't hold a sneeze. Let me see your register. (*Finds rabbit's foot*) This is my lucky foot. Say good-bye to yourself. You're going to be a changed man. (*Takes Liguras off*)

FIC DOE: Don't fall off the roof! Modem comfort needs a good shellacking. You two scare off somewhere. I'm going to buy myself something deluxe. Chin, chin! The folk mind converts the neutral to the negative. (*Exit*)

OLD MAN: (*Sotto voce*) We can anticipate an ugly document. (*Exit with Old Woman*)

Scene 4

(*Enter Karp and Nyla, dog tired*)

KARP: I'm dead, but I just won't lie still.

NYLA: You don't have to get rigid about it. Shoe repairs as usual.

KARP: Your conic sections don't lack verve. Front! (*Dinging desk bell*)

FIC DOE: (*Entering in Bunker's suit, mouthing an extravagant confection*) Don't have a hissyfit.

KARP: Do you know how to train fleas?

FIC DOE: I just take my work to lunch and do my job.

KARP: What did the dumbwaiter say to the silent butler?

FIC DOE: Er, I forget.

KARP: Puns are the antidote to memory. Where's Bunker?

FIC DOE: Why he's up — say, who wants to know?

NYLA: We're in business!

KARP: We're in the same business.

(*Enter Old Couple*)

OLD MAN: You must always grind forward.

OLD WMN: A neat hand leads to the top.

NYLA: Do you just talk that way, or does it take theories?

FIC DOE: They're on another channel. How about a nice room with a view? The night scene of diced firmament?

KARP: You miss my drift. Just point us in the right direction. We don't want to come between you and your appetite.

FIC DOE: (*Hand out*) I do my calling with a card. Continuity demands factory cash.

KARP: What you're hearing is the sound of a fifty-cent piece sitting on the counter.

FIC DOE: In a matter of syllables, a life of iniquity caught up with the former management. (*Reads from blotter*) "The subject was subdued and assumed the position."

KARP: Spell it out.

FIC DOE: The porter had sticky fingers. Bunker knows how to take care of help. He's giving a music lesson.

NYLA: That sounds like a reasonable generalization, of the sort of thing that tends to suggest the truth, but isn't.

             (*Enter Bunker with Liguras bound and gagged*)

BUNKER: In a few years the asylum will put you up for adoption and — (*seeing Karp and Nyla*) — the electric lights are back in their sockets.

KARP: What kind of vacation is this?

BUNKER: The great value in unemployment is time.

NYLA: Stop giving us the thermometer. You can't tell a mirage from a snake in the grass. Who put your clothes in circulation? The flea trainer with the push button mind. In your eyes shampoo is a rug treatment. He was dealing from the floor. I'd like to break into pictures too, but it was scholars who thought up aliases in the first place. Hands have as much personality as the face.

OLD MAN and OLD WMN: That's not our information.

FIC DOE:	Fictitious Doe tried to feel way out of spot. Dots polkaed before his eyes.
BUNKER:	There's always somebody else in the woods. (*Releases Liguras*)
FIC DOE:	The sky got full of zeros. He tried jumping through smoke rings.
LIGURAS:	I have you to thank for the underwater comedy, and you for the skin of my teeth.
NYLA:	Flowers cover everything. Lifesaving is temporary at best.
BUNKER:	Things in their places make the world turn. (*To Fictitious Doe*) You surrendered to economic compulsion. Look forward to an endless belt.
FIC DOE:	Fictitious Doe looked at his hands. They looked back to him like lizards.
OLD MAN:	Permanent recall.
KARP:	There's no escaping the ridiculous. But it's curtain time, my friends. Stage developments outweigh these numerical pastimes.
BUNKER:	My leisure moments have just begun.
NYLA:	Don't you think you're skating a little close to the pharmacy?

BUNKER: Being poor *is* sanitary. Meet me in the wings. (*Exit*)

LIGURAS: What's behind all that?

KARP: A more detailed treatise on the same subject.

OLD WMN: What is his field of endeavor?

KARP: Catching bullets with his teeth.

OLD MAN: The thought agitates my viscera.

LIGURAS: Some honeymoon.

NYLA: What makes men see worlds in us?

FIC DOE: Fictitious Doe began to focus on private planes.

Scene 5
(*Backstage at a theater*)

KARP: (*First sober, then giddy*) Being a spectator is the finest
            profession in the world. I'd like to show you my life,
            a headlong contraption of causeways over miasma,
            cornered by the weight of destination. Everyone has his
            reasons. I've never taken kindly to the hard work of a
            daydream; nature beat me to it. The high calling of the
            microbe hunter fell on deaf ears. You don't find logic in
            character. Approximating experience is a kind of model
            making, and vice versa. The genuine article has the
            nearness of blood and the play of extension cords. I may

harbor qualms, but wide loads outnumber points of interest, and the Junior League takes a back seat to storyboard romance any day.

BUNKER: (*Entering*) You've got quite an opinion of your drawing power.

KARP: The public wants a private moment. It's time we believed our own forecasts.

BUNKER: (*Sizing up*) My horseback guess is nothing material happened. If the sky recedes, get some sleep. Electricity delivers my needs.

KARP: We live by accidents of terrain.

BUNKER: Every swamptrotter has an alibi. We're here to shoot, not write our memoirs.

KARP: I'm allergic to caricature. Silly putty won't get you past jagged edges.

BUNKER: Powder your nose.

NYLA: (*Entering*) I'll take it under advisement. (*To Karp*) You ought to prohibit him from spreading gloom.

BUNKER: Any fool can put his pants on better than the wisest man can do it for him.

KARP: Clothing disguises the appearance of skin.

NYLA: (*To Bunker*) Do you ever meet with foul play?

BUNKER: An engine attracts a man to what is accurately called crime. The unit of currency is fear.

NYLA: Can we depend on the switch?

KARP: Things do stage periodic rebellions.

BUNKER: Life is a use of man in this spot.

NYLA: Undertones belie your optimism.

BUNKER: Events are never absolute. Their results depend entirely on the individual.

KARP: I can't live in a world without coincidence. Forever affable is no match for this company. I need a close-up of scenery. (*Exit*)

NYLA: What kind of gas is that? It smells like furniture remover.

BUNKER: Hat sauce. You're looking at a scorched man, trying to redeem his dismay — for hypnotic civility.

NYLA: No one's had their teeth pulled out. Rid yourself of guilt by knowing what's right.

BUNKER: Everything is addition and subtraction. The rest is conversation.

NYLA: It should sound more like understatement when you don't know the whole story.

BUNKER: History doesn't make mistakes.

NYLA: (*Carefully*) It ate a lot of sleep.

BUNKER: . . . You've observed too much silence.

NYLA: That black little thing's my nature embedding kit.

BUNKER: We live in bags all right. Otherhood supplies a birthday suit.

NYLA: Sleeping is not a way of life.

BUNKER: The right word still seems like the solution to any problem. Celebrities have always been drunk.

NYLA: That would be a hell of an idea, after we talked it out. But playing by ear is a pain in the neck.

BUNKER: Keep it up and you're out of business. Every time you pull it out of the fire there's less to pull. Drawing longevity pay is very complicated.

NYLA: Money's always wired to gratitude. Some don't make themselves a chive.

KARP: (*Entering*) How much is that in horsepowder? Why haven't you two got a title?

BUNKER: The public ears are very flexible.

NYLA: We want to lead our own lives.

KARP: Being born isn't everything. Take turns driving. Ride
            with the pun. You're better off inside.

BUNKER: I like the futility of effort.

NYLA: I never depend on mechanisms for happiness.

KARP: Long last looks must end.

BUNKER: Let's go on in amongst 'em. (*Exit with Karp*)

(*Suspense-filled minutes for Nyla. Touches Bunker's street-clothes. Sees
            past. Searches future . . . A loud shot. Animal eyes. More
            minutes.*)

BUNKER: (*Enters, ashen; grins, bullet in teeth; spits it out. Nyla
            breathes.*) The captain's trajectory was flatter than I
            calculated.

NYLA: There's a lot of oxygen in here.

BUNKER: I'm a little unclear of my movements tonight.

NYLA: You had a call from the dark side?

BUNKER: The skinny hand was on me. Cobwebs steam off my
            shoulders.

NYLA: Material fullness naturally flares. Fame peels away
            each reenactment. A note should be added for the
            beautiful drivers.

BUNKER: We work for years before millions and nobody knows
            who we are. Each town has its own inserts. When
            your whole life is depending on a bolt, you have a
            different respect for what you do. I get tired when I
            see normal people. You're killing yourself so they can
            say there's more where that came from. I don't have a
            death wish. I'm too far gone. On a day off my nerve's
            a wreck.

KARP: (*Entering with bankroll*) You've got hell's own drag
            with the life extension bureau.

BUNKER: I wouldn't be in my shoes without steps in that
            direction.

KARP: That equalizer is a dapper apparatus.

BUNKER: I'm not altogether stupid. But a change of
            temperature came over me. Machines are only
            interesting in being invented. Specific vocabulary
            makes philosophy handsome. It runs through nope
            endlessly.

KARP: (*Incredulous*) You, a partition specialist! Cue fate
            music.

NYLA: You have a right to an ideal, gaffed with large beans
            or not.

KARP: The voice of several waters.

NYLA: (*To Bunker*) Don't lament your education. We

binomials are so partial to things. Today's automatic will be tomorrow's manual. Periodic law rhymes your ingredients, but hesitation marks outfit a fugitive for still life. Only novels end when they feel like it.

KARP: Watch those curves.

BUNKER: (*To Karp*) Spend time getting ready to be dead and your reputation for aplomb is a cheap separation. You are rich in umbrellas. The gods especially dislike the smell of humans. Take it from one old creature. Any further concern you may have about yourself is luxury.

PARTICLE ARMS (Story Map)

Scene 1 (*Night, a city street*). Bunker, dressed for travel and carrying luggage, is attempting to slip out of town, but is intercepted under a streetlamp by his friend Karp, with whom he drinks several toasts. Karp tries to prevent his departure, and Bunker, a man of few words, tarries long enough to be surprised by Nyla, the last person he wants to see. It appears Bunker and Nyla have a history, whose recent events are not happy. Karp interjects facetious asides into their heated exchange. Despite Nyla's arguments, Bunker has made his decision and takes his leave.

Scene 2 (*Another town, hotel lobby*). Liguras, the seedy hotel desk clerk with a lousy personality, can't help bullying Fictitious Doe, the bellhop/janitor with a circular psychology. An old couple wanders in and out spouting apparent non sequiturs. The situation is upset by the arrival of Bunker, who cows Liguras, befriends the old couple, installs Doe behind the desk in Liguras's place, and retires to the roof.

Scene 3 (*Next morning*). Believing everyone asleep (in fact he is observed by the watchful old couple), Doe rifles Bunker's suitcase, where he finds a revolver and bullets, and appropriates a bright orange rabbit's foot together with some clothing. He wakes Liguras, and lords it over his former boss. Bunker recovers the suitcase, and mistakenly blames Liguras for the theft, much to Doe's pleasure. In a moment alone, the old couple drop their disguises and reveal themselves as anthropologists doing field research. Doe plants the rabbit's foot where it will incriminate Liguras, and the ruse appears successful when Bunker finds it.

Scene 4 (*Enter Karp and Nyla, dog tired*). Karp and Nyla arrive, searching for Bunker. While they question Doe, Bunker brings in Liguras for punishment. Nyla has seen through the old couple's disguise as well as Doe's unlikely tale, and tries to set things straight. Karp explains Bunker's curious profession: catching bullets with his teeth in a stage act. Karp is his manager and partner.

Scene 5 (*Backstage at a theater*). While Karp and Bunker prepare for the act, Nyla arrives. This time her talk with Bunker is less acrimonious. They seem closer to agreement over their past troubles, and over the dangers inherent in his line of work. While Bunker goes on stage to do his act, Nyla is left alone in the dressing room. She hears the shot. Finally Bunker returns, philosophical and somewhat dazed. The cynical Karp can't believe the change in his friend, but Bunker and Nyla seem to have reached some kind of reconciliation.

ADVENTURES IN POETRY (AiP) began publishing in 1968 as a mimeographed "little magazine," and continued through 1976 with individual pamphlets, featuring work by John Ashbery, William Burroughs, Allen Ginsberg, Bernadette Mayer, Frank O'Hara, James Schuyler, Anne Waldman and numerous others.

After a hiatus, AIP began again in 2000 with a series of books by both established and new innovative writers.

AIP books are edited by Larry Fagin and Christopher Mattison.

FURTHER ADVENTURES

The Cave: Clark Coolidge & Bernadette Mayer
978-0-9761612-5-7 / 7 x 10 / 80 pp. / $16.00

The Messianic Trees: Kit Robinson
978-0-9761612-6-4 / 6 x 9 / 312 pp. / $16.95

Situations, Sings: Jack Collom & Lyn Hejinian
978-0-9761612-4-0 / 6.125 x 9.25 / 200 pp. / $15.00

Enthusiasm: Odes & Otium: Jean Day
978-0-9761612-3-3 / 6 x 8.5 / 144 pp. / $15.00

Selected Poems 1965-2000: Merrill Gilfillan
978-0-9761612-2-6 / 5.5 x 8.5 / 144 pp. / $16.95

Baby: Carla Harryman
978-0-9761612-1-9 / 5.25 x 7.5 / 64 pp. / $12.50

At Port Royal: Chris Edgar
978-0-9706250-8-3 / 5.5 x 8.5 / 74 pp. / $12.50